IMAGES OF ENGLAND

NORTHFIELD
VOLUME II

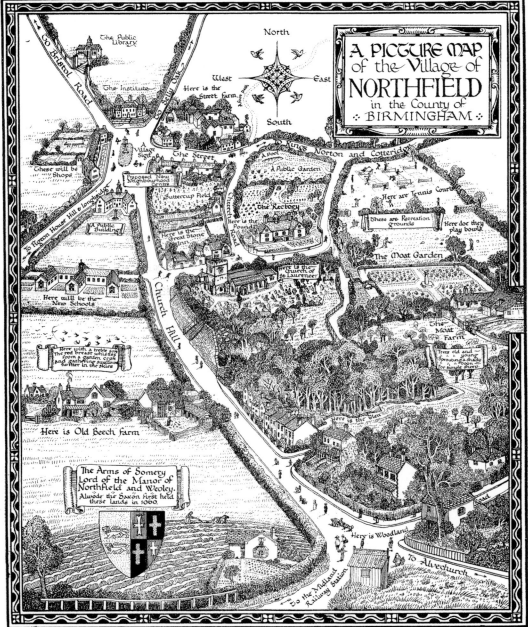

A PICTURE MAP
of the Village of
NORTHFIELD
in the County of
BIRMINGHAM

North

West   East

South

To Bristol Road

The Public Library

The Institute

Here is the Street farm

Village Sign

The Street

King's Norton and Cotteridge

A pool
A Public Garden

These will be Shops

Proposed New Neighbourhood Centre

Buttercup Field

The Rectory

Here are Tennis Courts

These are Recreation grounds

Here doe they play bowls

A Public Building

To Egron House Hill & Longbridge

Here is the Great Stone Inn

Here is the Pound

The Moat Garden

Here is the S.t Laurence

Here will be the New Schools

Church Hill

The Moat Farm

Here with a treble song the red breast will sing from a garden croft and gathering swallows twitter in the skies

Trees old and young sprouting sturdy anon for simple sheep

Here is the Glen

Here is Old Beech farm

The Arms of Somery Lord of the Manor of Northfield and Weoley. Alwode the Saxon first held these lands in 1060.

Here is Woodland

To Alvechurch

To the Midland Railway Station

Bernard Sleigh. del. Ivy. A. Ellis. scribe.   The Birmingham Civic Society.

IMAGES OF ENGLAND

NORTHFIELD
VOLUME II

MARTIN HAMPSON

TEMPUS

Frontispiece: A picture map of Northfield by Bernard Sleigh.
Published in 1921, it shows suggested plans for development.

First published 2003

Tempus Publishing Limited
The Mill, Brimscombe Port,
Stroud, Gloucestershire, GL5 2QG
www.tempus-publishing.com

© Martin Hampson, 2003

British Library Cataloguing in Publication Data.
A catalogue record for this book is available from the British Library.

ISBN 0 7524 3096 3

Typesetting and origination by Tempus Publishing Limited
Printed in Great Britain by Midway Colour Print, Wiltshire

Contents

Acknowledgements

I am grateful to Birmingham Library Services (Local Studies, History and Archives, Northfield and West Heath Libraries) for permission to use their photographs. Special thanks are due to the Bournville Village Trust (Diane Thornton) for the use of photographs on pages 19, 22, 23a, 41a, 49b, 51, 52-58, 77, 90b, 91, 97a, 113a, 123b; and to Cadbury Trebor Bassett (Sarah Foden) for 46b, 47a, 48a, 121b, 122, 123a, 124-125, 126a. The photographs on pages 29b, 118 and 38b are reproduced by kind permission of the *Bromsgrove Advertiser/Messenger* series. Acknowledgements are also due to the *Birmingham Post and Mail* for 12b, 86b and 120.

I should like to thank Martin Flynn for encouragement of this project in the early stages, and also the staff of Archives, Northfield and West Heath Libraries for all their help. I am particularly grateful to Brigitte Winsor of Archives for help with scanning, and would like to thank Local Studies staff for customary technical assistance.

Introduction

The current regeneration of the centre of Northfield, including the provision of improved shopping facilities and a new relief road, makes timely the appearance of a second Tempus book, looking at the area's recent and more distant past. The first volume – by my colleague, Pauline Caswell – has proved very popular since its publication in 1996. Some interesting photographs remained unused, and many more have been added to the library's collections since then. I have tried to make my selection complementary to Pauline Caswell's work, including new images of subjects previously touched upon, as well as introducing fresh topics.

Originally a Worcestershire farming village, in the Forest of Feckenham, Northfield appears in the Domesday Book of 1086 as 'Nordfeld' or 'northern clearing' (i.e. north of Kings Norton), having around 130 inhabitants, a priest, and 90 acres under cultivation. There was already a substantial stone church, parts of which still survive. The lord of the manor was William Fitz-Ansculf, a Norman knight, who also held estates at Frankley, Weoley, Edgbaston, Aston and Handsworth.

Although Northfield had its own manor house, close to St Laurence's Church, the lords of the manor resided at Dudley or Weoley Castle, no doubt leaving local administration to a bailiff. By the thirteenth century, the manor of Northfield covered a wide area, including the now separate districts of Bartley Green, Selly Oak, Selly Park, Bournbrook and Weoley Castle. St Laurence's Church served the whole of this area for centuries, until smaller parishes began to be carved out of it, from 1862 onwards.

For much of its history, the village of Northfield consisted of a scattering of farms and cottages, with the main community centred on St Laurence's Church. However, the upgrading of this part of the Bristol Road to a toll road, in 1762, encouraged housing development to the north and west, so that by 1840 this subsidiary settlement, extending along the main road and over to Bell Lane, was larger than the original village. From the sixteenth century, nailmaking provided an important addition to farm workers' incomes, and many of the newly built cottages had nailing workshops attached. Milling and quarrying were other local industries, later joined by claypit working and associated brickmaking.

Although the Birmingham-Gloucester railway was driven through Northfield in the 1840s, on a high embankment through the Rea valley below the church, it was not until 1870 that the village acquired its own station, and the inevitable consequence of gradual suburbanisation. The opening of the station was soon followed by the building of a number of railwaymen's cottages, a skating rink, shops and a temperance tavern. The railway made commuting into Birmingham possible for the first time, and commuter homes – both modest terraces and affluent semis – were soon lining a cluster of roads close to the station. In size, design and building materials, many of these houses were on a different scale from the simple country cottages previously characteristic of the area. These developments were reflected in the rise in local population – from 2,460 in 1851 to 7,190 in 1881, and almost 20,000 by 1900. Northfield became part of Birmingham only in 1911, by which time it was already established as an industrial, commercial and residential community.

The railway attracted new industry, again on a more ambitious scale than previously seen. Cadbury's chocolate factory in neighbouring Bournville (1879), the Austin motor works at Longbridge (1905), and Kalamazoo stationery works (1908) were all far-sighted enterprises, begun beside the railway, yet on greenfield sites with plenty of expansion room. All three had, directly or indirectly, a profound effect on employment and housing development in the area.

Lord Austin's successful ambition to realise 'motoring for the masses', with 400,000 Austin Sevens sold by 1939, led to the firm employing in its heyday between 20,000 and 30,000 workers. When his factory was founded, west of the Bristol Road lay mainly farmland, there were thirty working farms in the area, and 20,000 would have accounted for Northfield's total population. Between the wars, however, large council estates were built on the fields of Longbridge, Tessall and Allens Cross, with some accompanying private developments. By 1951, Northfield had 73,000 inhabitants, and much of the remaining farmland was subsequently built on in the 1950s and 1960s.

The unique Austin Village consists of 200 cedar wood prefabricated bungalows, shipped from America in 1916 to enable many wartime Austin workers to live nearby. The 'temporary' village is still there; and – once again thriving after a century of varied fortunes – the car factory remains vital to the local economy.

Although less directly influential as employers, the Cadbury's have exerted a profound effect on housing and environmental developments in Northfield. George and Elizabeth Cadbury lived for many years at Northfield Manor (actually a much enlarged eighteenth-century farmhouse). In true manorial style, however, they made their home a major centre of hospitality for business, political and charitable gatherings. They gave to the local community the Woodlands Hospital, Northfield Institute, Friends' Meeting House, and ultimately the manor house and park as well. Their establishment of the nearby garden suburb of Bournville greatly influenced estate design in Northfield. Much of the Shenley, Manor Farm and Hole Farm area was directly developed by the Bournville Village Trust, and the 1950s saw a notable collaboration at Shenley Fields between the Trust and Birmingham City Council. In this project, the Trust planned and built the estate, but offered the Council a number of tenancies in return for financial support. Housing for all ages was provided – flats, maisonettes and semis – at a time when the city was expanding rapidly and in urgent need of additional housing.

The Shenley development was also noteworthy for the involvement of five self-build housing societies, the residents themselves erecting 100 houses on the estate, including the community hall. The City Council's own local estates showed the influence of Bournville in their spacious layout and cottage-style housing.

For the Cadbury's, the setting of the housing was as important as the design; hence the Bournville Trust's emphasis on large private gardens and plentiful public parks. Here again, Northfield was strongly influenced by Bournville. The Valley Parkway, featuring preserved woodland, pools and streams and landscaped meadows, links the centre of Bournville directly with Northfield's own Victoria Common. Manor Farm Park, the gift of the Cadbury's, forms with Whitehill Common another linear park stretching towards Ley Hill, itself a former private estate given to the city by the Kunzle family, cake manufacturers. True also to the Bournville tradition, the historic centre of Northfield, centring on St Laurence's Church, was declared a conservation area in 1969.

Partly of Roman origin, and prominent throughout the history of Northfield, Bristol Road came into its own with the opening of a through tram service from the city centre to Longbridge (1923) and Rednal (1924). This development led to the road being substantially widened and re-surfaced, rapidly becoming Birmingham's premier highway, with its tree-lined pavements and a grassy central tramway reservation.

The Great Stone Inn and St Laurence's Church, *c.* 1900.

The lake at Manor Farm Park, *c.* 1960. This once formed part of the estate of Northfield Manor, former home of George Cadbury.

Commuting facilities were thus further improved, and the tram service became immensely popular for day trips to the Lickey Hills. The trams, supplemented by local bus services, helped to develop Northfield as a regional shopping centre – a role augmented in post-war years by much improved cross-city roads and more flexible transport facilities.

Being some six miles from the city centre, Northfield remains an important industrial and commercial community in its own right; yet it is also a popular residential area, whose striking mixture of old and new, urban and rural it is the aim of this book to represent.

one

Rural
Scenes

The view from the railway station in the 1920s, looking up Church Hill towards St Laurence's Church. Beech Farm fields and the stationmaster's house are on the left.

The stone from which the Great Stone Inn takes its name is seen here in its original position beside the inn, at the top of Church Hill in the 1950s, shortly before its removal for safety reasons to the nearby pound. It is an erratic boulder, one of many in the area, carried originally from the Arenig region of Wales by glaciers during the Ice Age, and deposited here as the ice retreated.

The summit of Church Hill, beside St Laurence's Church, showing Church Steps on the right and an eighteenth-century nailer's cottage straight ahead. This view from 1908 clearly shows remains of an ancient 'hollow way'.

A slightly later view of Church Hill, from 1921, showing a horse–drawn delivery van waiting beside Church Steps and the tower of St Laurence's Church rising through the trees.

The old village area around St Laurence's Church has enjoyed conservation status since 1969, and remains remarkably rural in atmosphere to this day, as can be seen from this view of the Great Stone Inn from across the well-tended churchyard, taken in 2003.

The Great Stone Inn, seen from Church Road on a late summer's evening, *c.* 1952, is a timber-framed house of fourteenth-century origin, encased in brick in the eighteenth century. It has served as a public house for at least 500 years.

Opposite above: The Old Rectory (demolished in 1933) is seen here from the junction of Church Road and Rectory Road, in 1921.

Opposite middle: Street Cottages, Church Road, 1921. These houses were formerly occupied by nailers, who were active in Northfield from the late 1500s. Many similar cottages were built in the village in the eighteenth century, often with a small forge attached. By 1727, there were 122 nailmakers here, many of them seeking to supplement their farm worker's wages. In what was essentially a family-based cottage industry, with long hours and low pay, Northfield specialised in large nails. Nailmaking did not survive the First World War, but these cottages lasted until 1964, when Great Stone Road was opened for through traffic.

Opposite below: Moat Farm and Tithe Barn stood, in 1921, just behind St Laurence's Church off Woodland Road. They took their name from a former moat that probably encircled the original manor house. The tithe barn was successfully converted into a house in the 1950s, but in 1969 it was demolished to make way for the Pine Walk development. The farm is remembered today in the road name Old Moat Drive.

Above left: The Tithe Barn, seen in 1950 before conversion, was probably built by the monks of Halesowen Abbey, who had close connections with Northfield Grange and the parish church. Of Tudor origin, it was built to store the farm produce collected by the church to augment their funds. A conservation order came just too late to prevent its demolition.

Above right: Paradise Cottage, Bell Hill, seen here around 1905, was another rural survivor. In this picture, Harriet Hemus can be seen with her daughter Ada Brown and grandchildren Eunice and Arthur.

This farm labourer's cottage just off Bell Hill still stood in the 1930s and served as a reminder of Northfield's rural past. In this transitional scene, recently-built semis rise in the background.

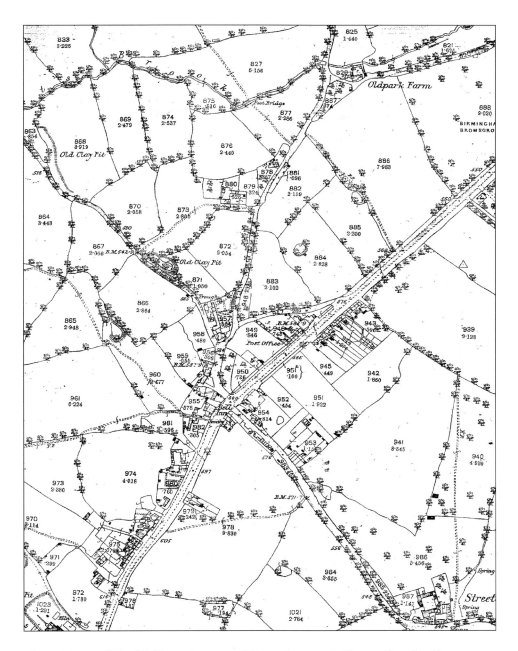

This 1884 map of Northfield reveals an essentially rural scattered village, with early ribbon development along the Bristol Road surrounded by fields. Although Roman in origin, Bristol Road gained its modern prominence when it became a toll-road in the late eighteenth century. This development encouraged new housing along the road, soon creating a second settlement that rivalled the old village round St Laurence's Church in size. The original centre lies to the bottom right of the map. By the First World War, the area between Bristol Road and the church contained much terraced housing; but the land to the north and west began to be developed only in the 1930s.

Bell Holloway in 2003 retains much of the character of an ancient 'hollow way', although it is in fact closely bordered by modern schools and housing. With its continuation, Merritt's Hill, it provides a direct, semi-rural link between Shenley Fields and Northfield shopping centre.

These former labourers' cottages at the junction of Merritt's Brook Lane and Merritt's Hill, seen here in the 1930s, still survive today. Although most of the farms in the area are now only a memory, the nearby Oldpark Farm still survives, although its land has now been built on.

Above: Yew Tree Farm, *c.* 1946. This stood facing Lower Shenley Farm across Shenley Lane, at the point where Shenley Green shopping centre and St David's Church now stand. The house and land are seen here shortly before the building of the Shenley Fields and Yew Tree Farm estates. This development was planned by the Bournville Village Trust in the 1930s but was delayed by the war until the early 1950s.

Right middle: Lower Shenley Farm is seen to the left and Yew Tree Farm to the right of this 1957 photograph taken from beyond Lower Shenley pond. Green Meadow Primary School now occupies a site adjoining the former farmyard, and Shenley Green Church and shopping centre lie to the left of the picture.

Right below: Lower Shenley Farm in 1957, shortly before its demolition.

This Edwardian view of the junction of Lickey Road and Bristol Road South, with the tower of the former Longbridge pumping station rising to the left, shows the rural area in which Herbert Austin established his motor works in 1905. The original factory lay to the right of the picture, facing the road junction; but the pumping station, built over a well with a 500-foot borehole, was also later used by the company. Constructed in 1893, the well could supply 500,000 gallons daily; but, once water was being received regularly from central Wales, it served only as a standby supply for surrounding districts.

Another view from about 1910, looking towards Birmingham. White Hill can be seen, with the Manor House estate (now Manor Farm Park) on the left.

Above: Another view of Bristol Road South taken around 1910, shows the entrance to the Priory on the right, with the undeveloped Shenley Fields area on the left still living up to its name.

Right: Hole Farm, *c.* 1930. This building is one of the few surviving farmhouses in the area, although like Oldpark Farm it has now lost its land. Of eighteenth-century origin, but built on the site of an older house, it was long the home of the Garland family (hence Garland Way). In the late 1950s, there was still no mains water and no electricity; there were just two gas points, a well, and a roof tank. The farmland extended from Bristol Road to Heath Road South. Although it is now mainly built over, hints of it survive in the fields and wooded areas of the Valley Parkway, and in the ornamental pool that was once the cattle pond. Hole Farm itself has recently been extensively modernised, and converted into apartments.

Hole Lane undergoing construction work in the 1920s, showing Hole Farm in a still essentially rural setting.

Hole Lane in the 1920s.

Right: A stile on Woodlands Park Road, on the walk between Northfield and Bournville in 1913.

Below: A bridge led from Groveley Lane, over the Birmingham–Bristol railway line, in 1925.

Coombes Lane, Longbridge, in 1937.

The now demolished Coombes Farm on Coombes Lane, was partly Elizabethan, and this 1937 photograph gives a clear impression that it was the kind of modest farmhouse once fairly common in the area. Before the First World War, Northfield had at least thirty working farms.

The site of Staple Lodge Road and Pitclose Road, *c.* 1930.

In the 1970s Ley Hill Recreation Ground and Merritt's Brook remained largely in their natural state. Originally part of the Ley Hill estate, the park was given to the city in 1952 by the Kunzle family, the cake manufacturers.

Cofton Road, at the Northfield/West Heath boundary, in 1936.

West Heath House on Alvechurch Road – a wintry scene from 1923.

two

Street
Scenes

Above: Church Hill in 1937, with Beech Farm (soon demolished afterwards) on the left. St Laurence's School can be seen behind the farm, with St Laurence's churchyard straight ahead. Before the churchyard, to the right of the picture are a row of former nailmakers' cottages. Beech Farm was of seventeenth-century origin, though encased in modern brickwork by the last tenant. A row of semis, fronted by a wide verge, now occupy the site.

Left: The same street in around 1996, looking downhill, with the churchyard and Church Steps on the left and the nailmakers' cottages beyond. The trees on the right of the picture occupy the site of the former Beech Farm.

Opposite below: The junction of Bristol Road South (Northfield's High Street) and Church Road, as seen in 1981. Before the 1930s shopping developments on the left, this corner site was occupied by the village smithy and several old cottages.

Above: Quarry Lane in 1937, appears to have been at a transitional stage. Although now a modern residential road, it occupies the site of an ancient quarry used by the Normans for the building of St Laurence's Church and Weoley Castle. According to tradition, quarried stones were conveyed direct to the church building site by a human chain. The quarry was exhausted by 1800, and was for many years overgrown by vegetation. The site was later filled in and occupied by the British Legion Club. Before the 1930s development, Quarry Lane was essentially rural, with two large houses, Quarry House and Quarry Farm – the latter being of Tudor origin.

The junction of Bristol Road South and Bell Lane in the 1980s. Although Huins' shoe shop no longer occupies the building on the right, this is often still referred to as Huins' Corner. The buildings on the left are among the oldest in Northfield; one was for many years a traditional butcher's shop, offering meat that was butchered on the premises.

The same road junction, again in the 1980s, but this time looking in the opposite direction towards Bristol Road. The prominent gabled building is the Bell Inn, an impressive Victorian pub which replaced a humbler predecessor, and was itself replaced by a much smaller and short-lived pub.

Pigeon House Hill, around 1920, looking towards Northfield shopping centre. The hill takes its name from the Pigeon House which formerly stood at the top of the hill on the left, and accommodated the servants to The Grange, a large house of Tudor origin, on the site of the present Longbridge Social Club just across the road. The Pigeon House kept pigeons to provide residents of The Grange with an alternative to salted meat during the winter months.

The Old Toll House on Bristol Road South – seen here around 1910 – stood opposite the junction with the present Lockwood Road. The Bristol Road was maintained as a turnpike road from 1726 until 1872. The Toll House was latterly used as a shop, being occupied for many years by George Hemus, the shoemaker and local historian. Like the Pigeon House, it was demolished in 1923 to allow road-widening for the planned tramline to Rednal and Rubery.

The junction of Bristol Road South and Chatham Road, *c.* 1920. Frank Hands' grocery shop on the right was for many years a prominent local business.

Bristol Road South in about 1925, looking towards the city centre. This image shows that much of Northfield's main shopping street at the time was still predominantly residential. Trams reached Northfield in 1923, extending to Rednal in 1924 and Rubery in 1926. Although for much of these routes they ran on a central reservation, this disappeared in the narrower shopping streets, creating hazards for other vehicles, and danger for passengers boarding or alighting in the middle of the road.

Bell Hill in the early 1970s, showing the newly-erected Grosvenor shopping centre beyond the houses centre left, and roadworks made in preparation for the (later abandoned) underpass.

Bristol Road South, Longbridge, close to the Austin works, *c.* 1914.

Longbridge Lane in 1945, showing the bridge over the river Rea.

Cock Lane (now Frankley Beeches Road) in 1934, showing the rear of the Black Horse Inn. The tall trees mark the line of a former lane-side hedge.

Tessall Lane, looking towards Hanging Lane. A transitional scene from 1935 it shows the first semi-detached houses beginning to appear.

Tessall Lane in 1935, taken looking towards the junction with Bristol Road. Recently-erected semis face a still unmade road and straggling lane-side hedge.

The junction of Tessall Lane and Hanging Lane in 1935, showing part of the former Tessall Farm on the left.

Tessall Lane, on the Longbridge/Northfield boundary in 1938 – showing a fully established residential suburb.

Bristol Road South, near the junction with Tessall Lane, in 1924, showing the recently laid tramlines.

Pigeon House Hill in 1923, near the junction with Hawkesley Mill Lane, showing tram-track laying in progress.

Egg Hill Lane, at the Longbridge boundary, 1944.

Felling elms at the Bristol Road South/Tessall Lane junction in 1979, with the King George V public house (now a restaurant) on the left.

Mill Lane, Longbridge, in 1958 showing the ford and footbridge, with the river Rea in flood. In the background may be seen the embankment of the Birmingham–Bristol railway, with a pedestrian tunnel leading through it to the Austin Village on the right.

Bristol Road South in 1931, showing a tram running down the central reservation that characterises much of the Rednal and Rubery routes. The mature trees on either side, giving a 'green', semi-rural feeling to long stretches of the road, are a prominent feature even today. This sylvan setting owes much to the influence of the Calthorpe estate and the Bournville Village Trust, whose land borders the first few miles of Bristol Road.

Bristol Road South by Manor Farm Park in the 1970s.

Bristol Road South near Hole Lane in 1962.

Bunbury Road, showing Bournville Village Trust houses shortly after completion in 1923.

Spiceland Road, on the Yew Tree Farm Estate, showing houses built by C.L. Holding for the Bournville Village Trust, shortly after completion, *c.* 1958.

The junction of Alvechurch Road and Lilley Lane, West Heath, in 1987.

Winter at Turves Green in the 1960s.

three

Houses and Housing

No. 6 Church Hill originally comprised two nailmakers' cottages, and was
converted to a single dwelling in 1958. The date of erection (1750), together with
the initials of the builder, appear in blue bricks on the east gable. In this 1970s
view the nearest part of the building is a single-storey former nailshop, which was
later used as a kitchen.

The same cottages, seen from St Laurence's churchyard in 2003, reveal a most
unusual feature. A projection to the chimney stack contains a tiled dovecote fitted
with four tiers of nesting holes. In this warm dry place, the pigeons would be
bred for food, supplementing the supply of pigs from the sty adjoining the
nailshop.

Street Cottages, on Church Road, seen here in 1934, were until their demolition in 1964 Northfield's finest group of nailers' houses. There were similar rows in Harborne and Bartley Green, most of which have now gone, though some individual houses survive. Northfield's best remaining row is on Church Hill, sensitively restored in keeping with their eighteenth-century origin.

Street Farm, Church Road, in the 1930s, faced Street Cottages. Originally holding 140 acres, extending to Hole Lane and Bristol Road, it dated from around 1700, and lasted till 1958. The YMCA building (opened 1961) now occupies the site.

Above: Northfield Manor, seen here in the 1970s, after its conversion to a university hall of residence, began around 1750 as Newhouse Farm, being first described as the Manor House in 1862 by its then owner, the Quaker registrar J. Edward Baker. The house was extended by Francis Atkins in 1868, and again by George Cadbury, who bought it in 1894. It never, however, had links with the medieval manor, and its panelling and Jacobean-style staircase were relatively modern.

Left: Elizabeth Cadbury beside the Manor House lake, *c.* 1950. As its name indicates, Manor Farm Park was originally farmland supplying produce to the 'Big House' itself, and to employees living on the estate. While the Manor belonged to the Cadbury's (1894–1951), it was used extensively for entertainment and charitable purposes, and following Elizabeth Cadbury's death the house became a hall of residence, and the park a public recreation ground.

Right: Although most closely associated with the nearby chocolate factory and garden suburb of Bournville, George Cadbury (1839-1922) lived for twenty-eight years at Northfield Manor House, making it a major centre for social, political and charitable gatherings of many kinds. Apart from their direct gift of the Manor House and Park, Woodlands Hospital, Meeting House and Institute to Northfield, the Cadbury family were also responsible for securing much of the nearby Lickey Hills for the people of Birmingham. The Cadbury influence on the development of Northfield continues today through the Bournville Village Trust, particularly in the design and layout of the Shenley, Yew Tree Farm, Manor Park and Hole Farm estates.

Below: Elizabeth Cadbury (née Taylor, 1858-1951), herself from an old Quaker family, married George Cadbury in 1888, and from the beginning assisted him in the development of Bournville, and later in the establishment of Northfield Manor House as a focal point for the furtherance of their political and social ideals. She herself was profoundly interested in the welfare of young people, whether it be through social organisations, educational reform, or health care. A particular concern was the Woodlands Hospital for Crippled Children, just across the road, which she visited daily, bringing bars of chocolate and often her pet parrot or donkey to amuse the patients.

Cadbury family group at the Manor House, *c.* 1910.

The Old Bell Inn, built in 1711, stood at the junction of Bell Lane and Bell Holloway, and in stagecoach days served as a midway station between the Hen & Chickens in Birmingham and the Rose & Crown at Rednal. Horses could be changed or rested here. When the line of the old coaching route was straightened, bypassing Bell Lane, trade was transferred to a new inn on Bristol Road. By 1839, it was known as Old Bell House, and remained a private residence until its demolition in the 1960s. There were extensive outbuildings at the rear, reflecting its former dual roles as farm and inn. It is seen here in around 1950.

The Davids, in around 1960, at the junction of Hole Lane and Bristol Road, was for many years the home of Laurence Cadbury (George Cadbury's son), who added two wings and laid out the extensive wooded gardens. In Laurence Cadbury's day, the house contained many big game trophies brought back from Alaska, North America and East Africa.

The Davids, c. 1989. Following the death of Joyce Cadbury in 1988, the house stood empty for a time, and was burned by vandals. It was subsequently demolished, and replaced by a housing estate of the same name, where the road Wynds Point commemorates George Cadbury's former country retreat at Malvern.

Left: Ley Hill House, seen shortly before it demolition in 2002, was at one time the home of Christian Kunzle, the cake and chocolate manufacturer, equally well known for his work for sick and disadvantaged children. The house and 40-acre estate were given to the city in 1952, and opened as a public recreational facility in July 1960.

An aerial view of Shenley Fields, taken in 1979, with Manor Farm Park to the right. Housing developments were planned in the 1930s on either side of Shenley Lane; but the war intervened, and it was not until the 1950s that the Yew Tree Farm and Lower Shenley Farm estates were built. Although under the overall authority of the Bournville Village Trust, Shenley Fields was built with the aid of various partnerships, including five self-build housing societies and Birmingham City Council (who were offered a number of tenancies by the Trust in return for financial assistance).

Opposite below: Ley Hill Miniature Golf Course was constructed in 1961, and for the next three decades proved very popular, 29,500 tickets being issued in 1974 alone. This 1966 photograph shows the rolling, wooded nature of Ley Hill Park, which provided an important green 'lung' in an area composed predominantly of interlinked housing estates. Following the closure of the course in 1995, the land was allowed to return partially to its natural state.

Yew Tree House, Shenley Lane, is seen here in around 1958, with the estate still in the course of construction in the background. This was, in fact, the former Yew Tree Farm on whose land the estate was built, and until the completion of the Shenley Green shopping centre across the road, a temporary general store was provided here.

The children's play area and bungalows for the elderly at Shenley Green are seen here in 1962, not long after completion. The Bournville influence is apparent here in the spacious layout, the cottage style of housing, and the retention of mature trees.

Early stages in the development of Lower Shenley farmland; laying the foundations of houses for letting, in Green Meadow Road, *c.* 1950.

Self-building on Green Meadow Road, in around 1953, under the auspices of Shenley Housing Association. Much construction work in Shenley was undertaken by local residents.

The junction of Green Meadow Road and Black Haynes Road in 1987, showing again the 'green', open layout, and the wide variety of housing made available.

Building houses to let, on Cyprus Close, Shenley Fields, in 1951, under the supervision of the Bournville Village Trust Building Department.

Above: This view of Spiceland Road, on the Yew Tree Farm Estate, provided, in 1963, a striking contrast to the cramped inner–city housing from which many Shenley residents had been transferred. Spiceland Road ran close to the site of the original Yew Tree farmhouse, and the area's rural past is respected by the retention of a long row of mature trees.

Right: Spiceland Road as viewed from Clun Road, in around 1958, again showing the presence of mature trees and the open 'village green' layout which is a recurrent feature of Bournville Trust housing.

Hole Lane in the 1930s, showing houses built in 1924. As in Bournville itself, the size of the gardens is a noteworthy feature. For George Cadbury, such gardens always had more than an aesthetic appeal; he highly valued gardening as a healthy recreational activity, which was also economically sound if fruit and vegetables were grown.

Hole Lane in 1976, showing houses built for letting under the 1974 Housing Act.

Garland Way, in 1979, was part of the Hole Farm Estate development begun in 1966, and was named after the family for long associated with the farm. Much of the building work in the area was undertaken by the Cornfield Housing Society, a co-ownership society sponsored by the Bournville Trust. In the centre of the picture, weeping willows mark the site of the former farmland ponds, which have been retained as a feature of the Valley Parkway, a 'green' pedestrian route linking Northfield with Bournville.

Cornfield Road, built by the Woodland Housing Society in 1927-8, is seen here soon after completion of the houses, still with open countryside beyond.

A view from 1966 of the junction of Heath Road South and Dinmore Avenue, showing owner-occupied houses built in 1960 by C.L. Holding & Sons.

Laurence Court, off Maryland Drive, consisted of twenty-two retirement homes, completed by the St Laurence Housing Association in 1983, shortly before this picture was taken.

Central Avenue, Austin Village, in 1918, shows some of the then recently erected wooden prefabricated bungalows shipped over by Lord Austin from Bay City, Michigan, USA, to ease a serious local housing shortage for his wartime workers. The conversion of the car factory to munition work had led to a vast escalation in the workforce, trebling by 1916 to 22,000. Wartime conditions made local bus and train services highly unreliable, yet there was a serious shortage of temporary accommodation within walking distance of the works. At a time of scarcity of labour and materials, such ready-made homes appeared the ideal solution.

Cedar Way, Austin Village, showing a children's octagonal play shelter and conventional brick houses built as a firebreak between the wooden bungalows. Within eleven months 200 red cedar bungalows were erected. Their internal layout was very advanced for the time, with built-in cupboards, bathrooms, inside toilets and central heating. Rents (including rates) were 18s (90p) per week. Though started as multi-occupied 'temporary' accommodation, the estate is still flourishing today. This 1920s view shows mature trees retained from the former farmland.

An aerial view of the 1930s council estate of Allens Cross, shortly after completion, showing still predominantly rural surroundings on every side.

Borrowdale Road, Allens Cross Estate, in the 1940s. Like many inter-war council estates, Allens Cross was influenced by the example of Bournville in its spacious layout and redbrick cottage style of housing. The estate is named after the former farm whose land it occupies.

Rimside, West Heath Road, in 1912, was one of the larger commuter houses built in the wake of the opening of Northfield railway station.

Heath House, West Heath Road, another large commuter home, contained, in 1926, a dining room with panelling from the demolished Christ Church, in the city centre.

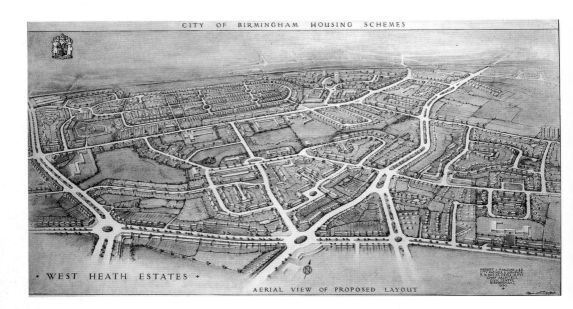

• WEST HEATH ESTATES •

AERIAL VIEW OF PROPOSED LAYOUT

HERBERT J. MANZONI C.B.E.
CITY ENGINEER & SURVEYOR
D. H. DAVIES, F.R.I.B.A. M.T.P.I.
CHIEF ARCHITECT
CIVIC CENTRE
BIRMINGHAM 1
1950

Above: An aerial view of the proposed layout of the West Heath council estates, drawn up in 1950.

Left: Hawkesley Farm Estate in the 1970s. The estate takes its name from a moated house of fourteenth-century origin, which was badly damaged in the Civil War, being held by both sides; it was later burned down and rebuilt in 1654. The farm formed part of the estate purchased by Lord Austin in 1916, although due to shipping difficulties prevailing during the war, no further prefabricated bungalows could be built on this site. The farmhouse was occupied for a time by Lord Austin's mother and sister, and later sold with accompanying land to Birmingham Corporation, who in 1958 designed a small estate of bungalows and flats, demolishing the house, but retaining its moat as a water feature.

four

Institutions

St Laurence's Church, *c*. 1900. Norman in origin, as one doorway and the lower stages of the tower reveal, it occupies the site of an earlier, Saxon church, probably of wood, of which no trace remains. Prominent later features include the well-preserved thirteenth-century chancel and panelled fourteenth-century timber porch.

St Laurence's Church, seen in 1909 from 'The Darky', an ancient bridle path following the east side of the churchyard. Still a fairly remote country church in the nineteenth century, it escaped a drastic Victorian restoration, remaining essentially medieval in character. In 1898–1900, G.F. Bodley added a north aisle in fourteenth-century style to match the south arcade.

Above: The interior of St Laurence's Church in 1930, looking towards the chancel which Pevsner described as 'the glory of the church' and 'complete and unspoilt'. Northfield was fortunate in having Henry Clarke as Rector from 1834 to 1880; for during his long ministry he restored many furnishings destroyed during the Reformation, including the fine chancel screen – all in harmony with the character of the building.

Right: The north chapel and organ of St Laurence's, 1941. The organ was given in 1937 by Lord and Lady Austin in memory of their son, who was killed in action during the First World War. It was rebuilt in 1983.

The Old Rectory at St Laurence's, shortly before demolition in 1933. Basically a medieval building, reconstructed in around 1705, it was replaced by a more modern house, which was in its turn replaced in 1976 by the present, much smaller Rectory. The 1930s Rectory was retained, however, as the Pastoral Centre, and a link with the original house survives in the form of a timber-framed barn of around 1700.

Revd Henry Clarke, Rector of Northfield for forty-six years (1834–80), did much to preserve and indeed enhance the character of St Laurence's Church. A keen follower of the Oxford Movement, which emphasised the Catholic teaching and sacramental nature of the Church, he restored many traditional features, including choir stalls and pulpit, chancel screen, sanctuary floor tiles, nave pews and stained glass windows. An 18ft cross stands in the churchyard in his memory.

Revd Reginald Haysom, Rector of St Laurence's 1923-45, is seen, in the 1930s, standing in the Rectory garden, with company including Miss Florence and Mr Osmond Stock, notable benefactors to the church and the local community.

A traditional scene of around 1920 showing St Laurence's Church, school and schoolmaster's house, with Beech Farm on the right. A charity school was founded by the Rector, Dr William Worth, as early as 1714, a purpose-built school being erected in 1837. A day school was opened in 1845, absorbing the charity school. There were eighty-one pupils in five classes at this time. By 1870 there were 114 children, with weekly fees between 1*d* and 6*d*.

St Laurence's School, *c.* 1970. The school was enlarged in 1890, 1898 and 1904; but steadily rising numbers led to classrooms housed in huts by the late 1920s. The school was reorganised as a junior and infants' in 1939; but further expansion led to classes overflowing into the church hall in 1951 and Northfield Institute in 1953. By 1961 there were thirteen classrooms and a school hall, and nearly 350 pupils.

Mr Smith's class at St Laurence's School, *c.* 1936. From 1952 the school had aided status. It acquired a reputation for inspirational teaching – for example, the former schoolmaster's house became a 'Little House of Numbers', used in maths lessons – but the overcrowded and rapidly deteriorating building necessitated a phased move to new accommodation in Bunbury Road, completed in 1972. The old school has been successfully adapted for housing.

Woodcock Hill Primary School, on Far Wood Road, *c.* 1960, was opened as a junior and infants' in 1954, being reorganised into separate junior and infants' schools in 1959. By 1961 there were fifteen classrooms and two halls.

Ley Hill Primary School, in around 1960, was opened as a junior and infants' in 1954. In 1961 there were fourteen classrooms and a hall. In this picture, the recently built Ley Hill Estate can be seen to the left of the school, with the trees of the newly acquired Ley Hill Park beyond.

Part of the Bell Holloway campus, shortly after opening in 1964. Bell Holloway brought together three special day schools founded between 1895 and 1929: Victoria School for the physically handicapped, Longwill School for the deaf and partially deaf, and the George Auden School for the partially sighted. Though in separate buildings, they shared many communal facilities, and enjoyed the latest in special equipment and teaching methods.

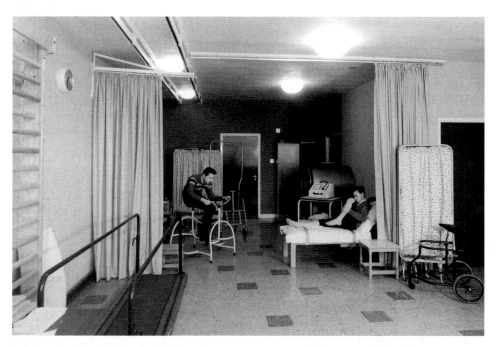

Inside Victoria School, Bell Holloway, *c.* 1965. The campus began with 300 children from all over South Birmingham and neighbouring parts of Warwickshire and Worcestershire. The George Auden School has since closed, to be replaced by another special school, the James Brindley.

A Bell Holloway science class (above) and school class (below), *c.* 1965.

Turves Green Primary School, seen soon after its 1938 opening as a junior and infants', housing 336 pupils. A senior department for 400 children was opened in 1939, and the junior and infants' was enlarged in the same year.

Turves Green School, *c*. 1940. The primary section expanded rapidly,192 pupils being housed in huts by 1944. The senior section became a separate secondary modern school in 1945. A new junior department for 480 opened in 1952; the old junior and infants' block was then used for infants only. By 1961 there were twenty-three classrooms and two halls.

Above: Turves Green Senior School playground in the 1940s. Following the reorganisation of the senior section in 1945, a new boys' school accommodating 420 was opened in 1953, and the old school used for girls only. In 1961 there were 970 boys and 660 girls.

Right: Domestic science at Turves Green Girls' School in the late 1940s; at work in the 'housewives' flat'.

Wychall Farm Primary School, on Middle Field Road, in around 1960, was opened as a junior school in 1956, and with infants in 1957. By 1961 there were fourteen classrooms and three halls. The school is named after a former farm whose site it now occupies.

A class in Wychall Farm School, *c.* 1960. Like many new schools of the period, its light and airy and spacious layout, with low-rise child-friendly proportions, seemed to embody post-war optimism, and provided a deliberate contrast with the often dark and fortress-like pre-war Victorian and Edwardian buildings.

Tinker's Farm children in the 1930s, wearing suitably modern uniforms for their new school. A junior and infants' school, housing 432 pupils, was opened in 1931 on the site of a moated seventeenth-century farmhouse of the same name. A senior department for 800 was opened in 1932. The infants had a separate building from 1937, and the senior departments became separate boys' and girls' secondary schools in 1945. In its early days, the school was regarded as a showpiece, and was much visited by educationalists.

Music lesson at Tinker's Farm School in the 1930s. The buildings were notably innovative, open-plan and open-air in emphasis, whole outer walls of classrooms being folded back in summer. The primary school closed in 1957; but the secondary school survived until 1986, being latterly known as Northfield School. The buildings were later used by community groups, and demolished in 2000 to make way for a housing estate.

Hawkesley Farm (or Alderman Bradbeer) Primary School is seen here shortly after completion in 1954. Opened as a junior mixed and infants', it had seventeen classrooms and two assembly halls. It was one of the first of a series of timber-built schools.

St Anne's Church, Alvechurch Road, West Heath, shortly after completion, *c.* 1970. The previous building, originally West Heath Mission, became the church hall.

St David's Church, Shenley Green, soon after completion in 1970. Built to serve the major post-war developments of Weoley and Shenley, its dedication to a Celtic saint was not only a tribute to the contribution made by the Welsh community within Birmingham, but was also a reference to the fact that Birmingham receives its water from Wales, and the Elan Valley aqueduct passes through the parish.

The interior of St David's, again in 1970. From the start, the building was planned to serve as a full community centre, with flexible furnishings that could be easily moved for musical or dramatic performances, and a large porch serving as a meeting and exhibition space. Seating was planned so that no one was more than 45 feet from the altar, with choir and congregation arranged in a wide arc around it. The building incorporates several stones which once formed part of the structure of St David's Cathedral in Wales.

St Bartholomew's Church, Allens Farm Road, was built in 1938 to serve the Allens Cross Estate, and is seen here soon after its completion. Its simplified redbrick Romanesque style, with harmonious whitewashed interior, was characteristic of the period. Following a serious fire in 1998, the church has been closed pending a decision on a new building.

The interior of Our Lady and St Brigid, seen soon after completion in 1936. A prominent landmark on Frankley Beeches Road, with its Italianate bell tower and simple redbrick round-arched style, its was built to serve the Roman Catholic community in the Allens Cross area. The apse, a 25ft domed recess behind the altar, has recently been beautified by the addition of a huge Renaissance-style mural of the Resurrection by Neil Harvey, which has taken nine years to paint. The adjoining St Brigid's Junior School was opened in 1950, and uses the previous church of 1931 as its assembly hall.

Above: The Priory, originally Gainsborough House, was built in 1862 as the home of the Stock family, dealers in steel and stained glass, and prominent local benefactors. A large house in extensive wooded grounds with a lake, adjoining the Woodlands Hospital, it was given by the family to the local diocese, who in 1905 offered it to the Order of Our Lady of Charity, who started a foundation there for the sick and disadvantaged. The Bristol Road entrance is seen here in around 1930.

Right: The Priory, *c.* 1960. The main building was gradually extended, eventually accommodating ninety women and girls. A laundry was opened to provide work for the residents and a useful source of income. Some laundry needs in the local community were met; but the Woodlands Hospital was the main customer.

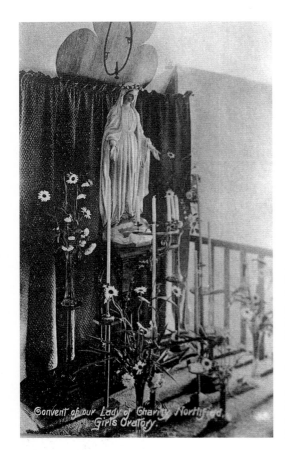

Convent of our Lady of Charity, Northfield. Girls Oratory.

Left: The Girls' Oratory at the Priory, *c.* 1930. Becoming too expensive to maintain, the Priory was demolished in around 1980 and replaced by a smaller and more easily managed building. Some of the land was sold, and Maryland Drive built.

Below: Nazareth House, seen here in around 1920, was opened on Lickey Road, Longbridge, as a Roman Catholic orphanage in 1912, and later converted to an old people's home. It was recently demolished, and the site developed as a housing estate.

Shenley Cottage Homes in the 1950s. The homes opened in 1887, and were paralleled by a similar development in Erdington, designed 'to separate the children whose unfortunate circumstances placed them in care, from contact with adult paupers in the workhouse'. Kings Norton Board of Guardians chose the site at Shenley as giving the children 'substantial benefits of pure country air, bright, cheerful and elevating surroundings', and freedom from 'the interference of undesirable relatives and friends'. Eight homes were built on this site, five more being added by 1936. Initially, the children were segregated from the community, being educated on the site; but from 1932 they began to attend outside mainstream schools. The division of the site into separate houses with foster parents marked an important advance on accommodation in huge anonymous institutions, and this concept was increasingly extended into the wider community, with an 'Uncle and Aunt' scheme linking individual children with private families. Corporate patronage was also developed, and the children were encouraged to join local youth clubs like the Stonehouse Gang. There were regular day trips, camps and seaside holidays. The homes were gradually closed down in the 1980s, in favour of more scattered homes and individual fostering. The last home, Pinewood, was vacated in 1987, and modern housing now occupies the site.

The Friends' Meeting House, seen in 2003, was built in 1930, at a cost of £3,400, on land overlooking Victoria Common donated by George Cadbury. Since 1892, meetings had been held in Northfield Institute, and the new hall maintained links with various local organisations and two Cadbury adult schools until quite recently.

An aerial view of the Woodlands, the Royal Orthopaedic Hospital, taken in the 1960s. Originally a private house, the Woodlands was given by George Cadbury in 1909 as a convalescent home for the Birmingham and District Crippled Children's Union.

Open-air wards at the Woodlands, *c.* 1930. In common with many institutions of that time, the hospital placed great faith in the invigorating powers of fresh air, especially for polio and TB sufferers, who were nursed all the year round in the open, with only a roof to shelter them from the elements. In severe weather, tarpaulins covered the beds, while staff worked in overcoats and scarves.

A closer view of the open-air wards, also in around 1930. In view of the Cadbury's twin concerns with health and education, it is not surprising that one of the earliest hospital schools was established here, in 1912 (officially recognised in 1914). By the nature of their illness, many of the children were long-stay patients at this time. With improving living and healthcare standards, however, the number of long-stay patients gradually declined, diminishing the need for the school. It survived, however, in modified form, until 1996.

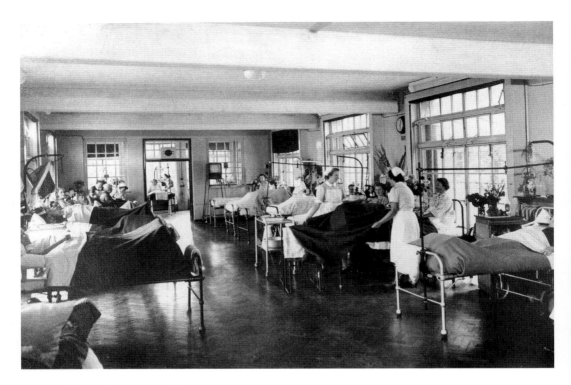

Above: The women's ward, Royal Orthopaedic Hospital, in the 1930s. The Duke and Duchess of York (later George VI and Queen Elizabeth) opened several new buildings in 1929, including a new children's ward, two adult wards, new operating theatres, a massage department, gymnasium, improved kitchens and staff accommodation. With the move towards general orthopaedic care, the hospital has steadily expanded, so that most of the extensive grounds are now occupied by buildings.

Left: The entrance hall to the original Northfield Library, showing in 1913 the delivery counter where books were issued under the old closed access system. The library, financed by Andrew Carnegie, cost £750 to build, and was opened in 1906. It proved short-lived, however, being burned down by local suffragettes in 1914. It was rebuilt the same year.

The newspaper room in the new library, c. 1930. Such rooms, with their large 'lecterns' supporting newspapers held down by metal strips, which the readers stood to read, were for many years a feature of all local community libraries.

Northfield Library in 1962. Although retaining the façade of the original building, it has been extensively modernised over the years, and extended at the rear towards Victoria Common. In this picture, the open-plan layout is in striking contrast to the rather forbidding 'cage-like' scene on page 84. The library is among the busiest in the city, issuing around 227,000 books a year.

Story hour at Northfield Library in the 1970s.

Christmas display at the library in 1976.

five

Work and Transport

The entrance to Kalamazoo in 1937, looking towards the Austin Village beyond the railway, with Mill Walk and the ford over the Rea in the foreground. The name Kalamazoo derives from that of the town in Michigan, USA, whose loose-leaf binding company supplied the Birmingham stationers Oliver Morland and Paul Impey, acting as their British agents. Deciding to produce their own binders, Morland and Impey moved from the city centre to Northfield in 1913. Beginning as printers of coloured wrappers and labels, they expanded greatly by making binders, extending the factory in 1919-20. A new factory was completed in 1962, and a successful Computer Services Division established in 1967.

Digbeth Mill, seen in 1929, gave its name to Mill Lane, and was worked originally by the adjoining river Rea. It was the manorial corn mill for Northfield, tracing its history back to 1278 at least, and linked in the eighteenth century to nearby Digbeth Farm (William Walker being tenant of both properties). The last tenants were the Morris brothers, who with the aid of a steam engine worked the mill till 1927, producing animal feed. After a period as a Public Works Department store, the mill was in ruins for some years, being finally demolished in 1958.

Above: The Fire Station, on the South Road/Bristol Road corner, is seen here soon after completion in 1959. Until 1911, when Northfield became part of Birmingham, the fire brigade was a volunteer force, and the station was originally at 146 Maas Road.

Right: George Hemus (1888-1973) worked for many years as a shoemaker at the Old Toll House on Bristol Road South. Having served his apprenticeship at Barnt Green at a starting wage of 4*s* 0*d* (20p) a week, he began his own business with a capital of 3*d* (1.5p), making boots by hand at 14*s* 6*d* (72.5p) a pair. In 1963, he published a short history of Northfield.

Shops on Bristol Road South in 1954.

Post office and shops on Heath Road, 1954.

Slater's general store in Yew Tree House, Shenley Lane, *c.* 1960, offered a temporary service until Shenley Green shopping centre was completed. Then this building (the former Yew Tree Farm) was demolished.

Shenley Green shopping centre, seen in 1963, was built opposite Yew Tree House. In this view, taken not long after completion, the church hall can be seen on the right. This was used regularly for services until St David's Church was built.

Shops at The Fordrough, West Heath, in 1959.

The West Heath café and stores, on Redhill Road, Kings Norton/Northfield boundary, *c.* 1930.

Herbert Austin (1866-1941) served his engineering apprenticeship in Melbourne, Australia, subsequently managing several small factories there, and returning to England with his Australian wife in 1890, to manage the Wolseley Sheep Shearing Company in Birmingham. Wolseley diversified into bicycles and machine tools, and were persuaded by Austin to try motor car manufacture. Austin exhibited his own first car as early as 1896, and in 1905 left Wolseley to set up his own factory in a derelict building in the fields of Longbridge.

By 1930, thanks to successful car production and a major contribution to the war munitions effort (for which he was knighted), Austin's factory had greatly expanded, as this aerial view reveals. At the top of the picture, to the right of the railway, may be seen the Austin Village, which consists of 200 cedar prefabs, shipped from America in 1916 to provide temporary accommodation for the massively increased wartime workforce. Below the Austin Village, to the right, may be seen the moated Hawkesley Farm, where Austin's mother and sister lived for a time, and whose moat now forms a central feature of a modern housing estate.

The main entrance to the Austin Works in the 1920s.

The body shop of the Austin Works in the 1920s. Herbert Austin was a 'hands-on' employer, priding himself on being able to do everything his workmen did. On his frequent tours of the workshops, if he saw a man bungling his work, he would step in and show him how it should be done.

Another 1920s view of the body shop in the Austin Works.

The Austin chassis assembly line in the 1930s.

Finishing work on A40 'Devon' saloons, *c.* 1950.

Austin Seven body and chassis about to be united, *c.* 1963. The 'baby' Austin, launched in 1922, had by 1939 sold over 400,000, doing more than any previous model to popularise motoring in this country. Relaunched in 1959, it became popularly known as the Mini.

Longbridge car workers catching trams home in the 1940s.

Longbridge railway station, 1954, looking towards Halesowen, with the Austin Works enjoying direct access. The Halesowen branch ran from Old Hill, on the Stourbridge Extension Line, to the Midland main line at Longbridge. Opened in 1883, its regular passenger service to Longbridge ceased in 1919, although workmen's specials to the Austin factory continued until 1964, formal closure taking place on 6 January. The present Longbridge Station was built half a mile away on the main line, and opened in 1978 as part of the Cross City service.

Northfield railway bridge during widening in 1894. Although the Birmingham–Gloucester railway had run through Northfield since 1840, a station was not opened here until 1870. The embankment is breached by two railway bridges at this point, giving access to Quarry Lane and Church Hill. Following the opening of the station, commuter housing grew rapidly on both sides of the embankment, which forms a physical boundary between Northfield old village and the West Heath/Turves Green area beyond.

Looking down Pigeon House Hill towards Longbridge and the Lickeys, on 7 May 1924, showing the recently laid tramlines. A tram service between Birmingham and Northfield had been operating since 1 October 1923, and was extended to Longbridge on 17 December of that year. The full route through to Rednal and the Lickeys had been opened on 14 April 1924, shortly before this picture was taken.

Construction work on Bristol Road South in association with the new tram track, 1925. The tram service to Rubery was opened on 8 February 1926, being the last part of the Bristol Road group of routes.

Laying the tram track on Bristol Road South, Longbridge, in 1925.

The Longbridge tram on the 72 route through Bristol Road, Northfield, running along the central reservation in the 1930s.

A tram on the 70 route, the service for Rednal and the Lickeys, passes along Bristol Road in the 1930s. This service was exceptionally popular with day trippers between the wars. On Bank Holidays, trams would carry passengers away from Navigation Street at the rate of 100 a minute. The journey took 50 minutes, and cost 5*d* (2p) when the service began in 1924.

Above: A Rednal tram, on the return journey to Birmingham, passes the junction with Hole Lane and a sign for an ARP shelter on the left, *c.* 1940.

Right: A Rednal bus passes by the Austin Works, on the final Lickey Road stretch, churning through the melting snow, in December 1956. The last trams ran along the Bristol Road routes on 5 July 1952, and were replaced by buses the next day.

Left: Demolition of shops and flats at The Fordrough, West Heath, in 2000, preparatory to redevelopment.

Below: The 'Bath Tub' (West Heath Lido), after conversion to a radio factory in 1940. Opened in 1937 as a huge entertainment complex, with a 180ft by 90ft swimming pool, café and ballroom, and 11 acres of grounds containing a putting green, archery lawn, children's playground and open-air stage, the enterprise never fulfilled its great promise, going bankrupt within three years, and being subsequently taken over by Stratton Ltd, producers of radio components and equipment, whose city centre factory had been bombed.

six

Leisure and
Sport

Church Road, with Northfield Institute on the left, *c.* 1920. Built in 1892 by George Cadbury, the Institute housed a coffee tavern, assembly hall, schoolroom, billiard room, skittle alley, kitchen and caretaker's house. For thirty-five years it served as the local Friends' Meeting House, and from the beginning as Northfield's adult school – a particularly popular facility, in view of the scanty schooling many adults had at that time received. A true community centre, it was for long the venue of whist drives, concerts, lectures, public and political meetings. The Institute was taken over by the City Council in 1951, and still functions as an adult education centre.

The caretaker started a youth club at Northfield Institute in 1921. The club appears here in 1944.

Northfield Institute Youths' Cricket Club, champions of Birmingham Joint Youth Clubs in 1942.

Northfield Institute Youths' Football Club, winners of the Birmingham Youth League South Senior Division 1945/46, and the Norman Chamberlain Cup.

Northfield Institute Football Club, winners of Kings Norton Junior Cup III Division 1939/40.

Girls' football match at Colmers Farm School, 1972.

Northfield Prize Band, with St Laurence's Church in the background, 1900. The bandmaster at this time was Braithwaite Llewelyn Fewster, the village schoolmaster. The band were three times winners of the Annual Crystal Palace Brass Band Competition.

Above: Northfield Prize Band, 1937. They rehearsed at Northfield Institute, and on special occasions would lead processions from the building to Victoria Common. The bandmaster at this time was Frank Wise.

Left: The Great Stone Inn, seen in 1888, has been a pub for at least five centuries, originating as a fourteenth-century timber-framed hall-type house of three bays. One bay was later removed to make way for the pound, and the remaining building encased in brick in the eighteenth century. It possibly began as the parish ale-house, serving members of the congregation who had made a long trek to the church from outlying parts of the parish. In the seventeenth century, it also served as the Coroner's Court, and as an administrative centre under Cromwell. In the 1851 Census, the landlord was also a butcher, such dual roles being common at the time.

The Great Stone Inn and pound in 1921. The pound, of at least fourteenth-century origin, was used by the Lord of the Manor for confining stray animals – a constant problem when there was much common land, unenclosed and poorly fenced fields. Owners would, on proving ownership, have to pay a fine to the Lord of the Manor. Bulls, oxen, cows, horses, pigs, boars, sheep and a swarm of bees have all been kept in this sandstone pound – one of the best preserved in Britain.

The Traveller's Rest, seen in 1927, shortly after completion by the Birmingham architect C.E. Bateman, was built of stone in a harmonious Arts and Crafts design on the site of an earlier pub, itself on the site of a former Nonconformist chapel. The original thatched roof soon caught fire, and was subsequently replaced by slate. This pub is likely to disappear in current plans for a new relief road.

The second Bell Inn, Bristol Road, in the 1920s. In 1790, the Bristol Road was straightened, thus bypassing the Old Bell, the original coaching inn on Bell Lane. A new Bell Inn was built on the new road in 1803-4, being itself replaced by a larger and more ornate building in 1897-1901. This in its turn was replaced by a small corner pub regarded by the brewers as more economical; but this was short-lived, and has now been converted into shops.

The second Black Horse, in around 1900, a late Victorian replacement of the previous house, and typical of the fairly ornate purpose-built pub which often replaced a semi-rural, simple predecessor. Improved transport links were rapidly suburbanising Northfield; hence the style of this new pub, which is essentially urban in character.

The third (and present) Black Horse, soon after completion by C.E. Bateman in 1929. A masterpiece of the Arts and Crafts style, it deliberately imitates a medieval manor house in form, its rambling layout suggesting evolution over a long period. There is much intricate wood and stone carving, including a half-carved chimneypiece, the carver of which died before completing, and a large beer garden and bowling green at the rear. This was very much a 'reformed' pub, aimed at appealing to the whole family.

The Beeches, on Hogg's Lane, Allens Cross: a 1930s view, shortly after completion, with open fields visible on the right.

The Longbridge Hotel, contemporary with the Beeches, and again built to serve new housing. Both pubs are typical of the 1930s Neo–Tudor style, which aimed to create a local landmark, respectable in image and wide in appeal.

Northfield Swimming Baths in 1978. They are currently being restored.

Tenants of Shenley Fields building their own community hall on Burdock Road in 1958.

Hampstead House Retirement Club, West Heath, 1987.

Shenley Fields Leisure Gardens in the 1970s.

Boating on the Manor Pool in the 1930s.

Ley Hill Miniature Golf Course in 1966. Formerly part of the estate of the Kunzle family, it was laid out in 1961 and lasted until 1995.

Victoria Common, seen in 1966, was first opened to the public in 1897. Formerly known as Bradley Field, it was once one of the village's open fields where, in the middle ages, individual villagers held strips of land divided by deep furrows, creating a corrugated surface called 'ridge and furrow', still traceable today.

Victoria Common, again in 1966. As part of the current regeneration of central Northfield, the sporting facilities here are to be considerably improved, with upgraded tennis courts, football pitches and bowling green, and a brand new all-weather pitch providing opportunities for various sports.

On 25 October 1953, the Northfield branch of the Ancient Order of Druids planted an oak sapling (an emblem of their order) as a natural memorial to the Coronation of Elizabeth II. In full regalia, and carrying symbolic crooks, they conducted an hour-long ceremony of 3,000 words, starting with the lighting of a mystic flame, and marked by the sprinkling of water from the Isle of Anglesey on wood-ash from Stonehenge. The sapling, from the Forest of Arden, was blessed by the Chaplain of Northfield Lodge, and hymns were sung.

Opposite above: The official opening of West Heath Recreation Ground in 1964.

Opposite below: The audience at the official opening.

Above: The visit of Right Revd Laurence Brown, the then Bishop of Birmingham (1969–77), to St Laurence Infants' School in 1973.

Left: The visit of Bishop Laurence Brown to Northfield Library, to see the special 'New Initiative' exhibition, March 1974.

Fancy dress contestants at the celebrations of the Coronation of George V, held in 1911 in Green Close, then an open space between Bristol Road and Maas Road, often used for local events.

George and Elizabeth Cadbury with a group of Austrian refugee children, at Northfield Manor House in 1921. The children had spent a year in Bournville following the devastation of their country in the recent war. The Cadbury's were particularly concerned with the plight of refugees, also helping a number of Serbs to settle in Birmingham.

Young Cadbury employees enjoying the hospitality of George and Elizabeth Cadbury at Northfield Manor, *c.* 1911. Apart from regular entertaining at the Manor House itself, the Cadbury's erected a barn in the grounds for the reception of large-scale gatherings such as this. In addition to Cadbury employees, vast numbers of children were entertained in the barn, especially the sick or disadvantaged, for whom Elizabeth Cadbury had a particular concern.

A scene outside the Manor Farm barn, on the occasion of the same visit by young Cadbury employees, *c.* 1911.

Elizabeth Cadbury welcoming Cadbury sales representatives and their wives to Northfield Manor House on 27 June 1935. A garden party was held in honour of the annual conference being held simultaneously at the works.

Some of the 600 guests going out into the grounds, where tea was served in two large tents, and two plays were performed in a huge marquee – Clifford Bax's *Square Pegs* and Bernard Shaw's *Dark Lady of the Sonnets*.

The visitors chatting in the Manor House grounds, preparatory to an evening dance at the works.

A close-up view of the Manor House and the sales reps' party, 1935. This visit typified the Cadbury's treatment of their workforce almost as part of an extended family.

Children from Vauxhall visiting Northfield Manor House on 24 June 1938, which also happened to be Elizabeth Cadbury's 80th birthday. Such parties from the inner city areas were organised by the Severn Street Friends' Meeting. They would be brought to the Manor Farm barn for a meal and games, and taken on a tour round the pool and gardens. This was the nearest many children came at the time to seeing the countryside.

Family group at The Davids, the home of her son Laurence, on the occasion of Elizabeth Cadbury's 90th birthday, 24 June 1948. In the morning, the flag station at Bournville Works had spelt out the message 'Greetings from us all', and flying alongside were the flags of many countries, symbolising her international interests. A deputation from the works conveyed their congratulations, bringing with them to the Manor a chocolate-covered birthday cake, decorated with marzipan roses, and a bouquet of sweet peas.

Elizabeth Cadbury celebrating her 92nd birthday at the Manor House, 24 June 1950. Sixty years before, when she married George Cadbury, Bournville was less than ten years old, and there were no more than 1,000 employees at the works. By 1950, there were 9,000 employees, and the estate had grown to 1,200 acres. Her particular concern had been to foster the growth of educational and healthcare institutions in the area, while also continuing her late husband's housing reforms. In her time, the Selly Oak Colleges, Bournville schools and Woodlands Hospital had all flourished, while on an international stage she had done much to advance the cause of human rights, world peace and the role of women in society.

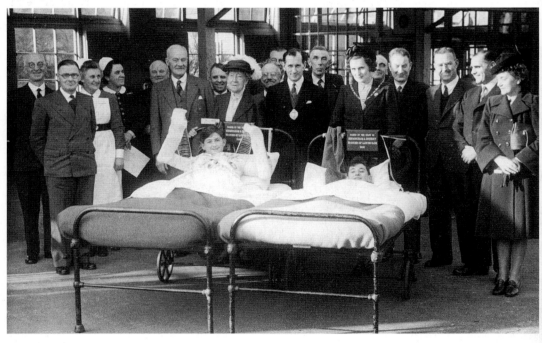

Unveiling of Lloyd's Bank beds at the Woodlands Hospital, 1948. Behind the left-hand bed, welcoming the sponsorship, is Elizabeth Cadbury, with, to the right, the Lord Mayor and Lady Mayoress, Councillor and Mrs J.C. Burman. This year marked the transfer of the Woodlands to the National Health Service; but, as an original donor of the building, Elizabeth Cadbury retained a close personal 'hands-on' interest in it, continuing to visit the patients regularly and stressing the need to maintain a caring individual approach under the new regime.

Concert at Tinker's Farm School in the 1930s.

Tinker's Farm Nativity Play, Christmas 1948.

The wedding of Zeta, daughter of Lord Austin, to Charles Lambert, himself a motor engineer, took place at Holy Trinity Church, Lickey, on 17 July 1928. The family group is pictured here at Lickey Grange, for many years the home of Lord and Lady Austin (and later a school for the blind). Zeta Lambert later published a book on her father, *Lord Austin – the Man* (1968).